S0-ABQ-590

GUY to GODDESS

GUY to GODDESS
An Intimate Look at Drag Queens

Photographs by
Rosamond Norbury

Text by
Bill Richardson

Whitecap Books
Vancouver/Toronto

Photographs copyright © 1994 by Rosamond Norbury
Text copyright © 1994 by Bill Richardson
Whitecap Books Ltd.
Vancouver/Toronto

All rights reserved. No part of this publication may be reproduced,
stored in a retrieval system, or transmitted in any form or by any means,
electronic, mechanical, photocopying, recording or otherwise, without
prior written permission of the publisher.

The information in this book is true and complete to the best of
our knowledge. All recommendations are made without guarantee on the
part of the author or Whitecap Books Ltd. The author and publisher
disclaim any liability in connection with the use of this information.
For additional information please contact Whitecap Books Ltd.,
351 Lynn Avenue, North Vancouver, B.C., V7J 2C4.

Edited by Elaine Jones
Cover design by Gek-Bee Siow
Interior design by Warren Clark
Cover photograph by Rosamond Norbury
Typeset by Warren Clark
Special thanks to Margaret Ng
Printed and bound in Canada

Canadian Cataloguing in Publication Data

Norbury, Rosamond.
    Guy to goddess

    ISBN 1-55110-254-4
        1. Transvestites—Pictorial works. 2. Transvestites.
I. Richardson, Bill, 1955- II. Title.
HQ77.N67 1994   306.77   C94-910420-5

For Barbara Beeby—
still ineffable,
still my best friend.

ACKNOWLEDGMENTS

In opening their closets—and their makeup cases—Miss Adrien, Carlotta, Mikki Diamond, Diana Rose, Richelle, Wanda Wacko, Scarlett, Studio, Tara Nova and Wanda Fuca made my sojourn possible. Lyn Guy offered service above and beyond the counter. At the House of No Guilt, a tip of the wig from Rose Bush to Judy, Barbi Diamond, Marleva, Gardenia, Leeza and, fairest of them all, Bonnie "Zip" Jealous. Craig Russell offered us the illusion for all too brief a moment and deserves to be remembered always. For allowing the butterfly to be observed in full, beautiful flight rather than nailing her to the specimen board, Bill Richardson has my true admiration.

—Rosamond Norbury

Thanks to Rosamond Norbury for her patient guidance, reassurances, and bold images; and most especially to the talented and generous artists who gave me the loan of their stories: Adrien, Andrew, Arin, The Big Wigs (Andrew and Steven), Carl, Wanda, and to the many other performers, aficionados, and observers whose insights and anecdotes found their way into this text.

—Bill Richardson

INTRODUCTION

I remember:

Teetering around my parents' bedroom in my mother's high heels.

Trying on her dresses.

Smearing her lipstick in a God-awful mess all over my mouth.

Admiring the expert way she could apply that same lipstick, perfectly, and without relying on a mirror.

Covert browsing through glamour magazines at the drugstore.

Getting the soundtrack to *Call Me Madam*, learning all the words to Ethel Merman's songs, and mouthing them with considerable ferocity in front of the bathroom mirror.

Watching Barbra Streisand's early television specials with an intensity the other boys in my neighborhood reserved for *Wide World of Sports*.

Apprehending that I would never achieve what I truly wanted, which initially I thought was to marry Barbra Streisand but which I soon realized was to *be* Barbra Streisand.

Figuring out, around the age of ten, that these behaviors were not socially sanctioned, and cauterizing the impulse. Nipping it in the bud.

Enlisting in the army of the outwardly normal.

Time and willfulness have done their work. Every so often, I have donned a frock at a party and flounced around
a bit. But I do this with all the skill and effect of a gro-
tesque and hairy football player at a frat party. I make an
artless woman; and that longing with which I was once
inhabited is dead and done. I have wondered how things
might have differed, had I been possessed of greater psy-
chic resiliency in my childhood. Had I had the guts to
follow the dictates of my nature, rather than the stric-
tures of nurture, would I be the stranger to rhinestones
I am today?

I have seen a great many drag shows: some entertain-
ing, some embarrassing, some brilliant, some ho-hum.
From a distance, I have admired drag queens for their
artistry and inventiveness, their courage and tenacity;

I design my entire outfit. I create a complete look. I can't imagine going to the mall to pick out a few little things to mix and match. For me, that would be a sin.

Drag Tip 1

If you're out of facial powder,
baby powder will do as well.

admired their involvement in gay community causes, the tireless fund-raising, most particularly for AIDS support services. But I have been intimidated by them, too; cowed by the varnished acidity, the bitchiness, the occasional outright meanness that is so often part of the onstage drag persona. Maybe I have been jealous, a little, seeing in their ebullience and willingness to fly in the face of convention a glimmer of a freedom and courage I wish I owned.

Films like *Mrs. Doubtfire*, and *Orlando*, and *The Crying Game*; the popular successes of performers like RuPaul; and the ongoing smudging of gender roles have all moved drag away from the margins and a little more into the mainstream. Nonetheless, if it were permissible for men to wear dresses and heels, they would surely do so in

greater numbers than is now the case. It requires a particular singularity of purpose for a man to build his life on a foundation of paint, gowns, wigs, and accessories. This is not a society that applauds those who thumb their noses at conformity; nor is outward diversity celebrated. What I mean is, drag takes guts.

I hope that some of the courage and outright ballsiness of the drag queens comes through in these renderings of their stories. Originality, humor, intelligence, longing, determination, and sometimes sadness; these are the qualities and traits I observed or intuited from our meetings and conversations. Observation, intuition, and conversation are the basis of this text, rather than analysis and scholarship. Much has already been reported, and there is much yet to say, about drag society and history, both of which are complex. These are the idiosyncratic

For me, drag isn't about passing as a woman. It's about being big. About exaggeration, and creating a character, and turning heads on the street. Mostly, drag is about having a blast!

Drag Tip 2

**Never wear blue eye shadow.
It's unforgivably tacky.**

observations of a curious tourist with a loose itinerary
and an agenda that was anything but fixed.

Drag is its own country. For a while, I traveled there,
learning this and that in a haphazard way by talking infor-
mally with some of the locals. I'm happy I went, and happy
to be home again. All travel is, by definition, unsettling.
It is particularly so when you are a tourist in a country
where you think you may have been born, a country full
of strange familiarities, where you wake up and know
you have been dreaming in the language, but where you
can never, not in a million years, ever come to live.

GUY TO GODDESS

WEDDING

Ask Adrien and he knows.

How many pairs of shoes?

Fifteen. Fifteen pairs of pumps.

Only fifteen?

I'm not what you'd call a shoe queen. I figure all I really need are gold, silver, red, black, and white. I'll have a couple of each, maybe a few more in black. I take a woman's size nine, so it's easy for me. I can go to any department store. Some guys need size sixteen or seventeen. They have to get them from companies that cater to cross-dressers.

How many wigs?

Drag Tip 3

Never wear rhinestones with satin. They claw. Rhinestones and lace can be problematic for the same reason. Also, be cautious when wearing a sequined jacket or top in tandem with a long wig.

Two hundred and thirteen. I counted them the other day. Wigs are really my thing. I like being a redhead. I like being fire and spice. I hate being a blonde, which is very strange because blondes are what I do best. Marilyn, Dolly, and Bette. Bette Midler, I mean. I've just started doing Bette.

How many dresses?

Gowns. A hundred and seventy-two. I'm working on my hundred and seventy-third. I'm making it for Bette.

Do you remember when you got your first dress?

Gown. When I was a little kid. Every Saturday, my

mom and my sister and I would go down to Frenchy's. That's a second-hand clothing place back home. You could buy a wedding gown for a buck. So I did. I had about twelve of them. I've always liked wearing white.
When did you learn to sew?

When I was twelve. I told them at school that I wanted to take sewing. They told me I couldn't. No boy ever had. I had to take industrial arts like everyone else. I said, Fine. I put on my little white hat, and my little lace gloves, and everything else that was white, and I went and sat in the woodworking classroom. I went there first thing in the morning and I just stayed there all day long. That was all I did. I just sat there. I said, You want me to take industrial arts? Then fine. Here I am, in Industrial Arts. And I'm not budging. Finally, they let me take sewing.

A lot of the queens I know come from small towns where there weren't many options. After a lifetime of being repressed, it's easy to understand the appeal of drag. You've got a dressing room, you've got a costume, you've got a stage, you've got an audience. You've got options. You can be anything you want. You can be a star.

We lived in the country, a really tiny place, but no one gave me a hard time. They were scared of me, I guess. When I was little, my one good friend was my horse. I'd put on my wedding gown and run through the fields, trailing this pink sheet I stole from my sister's bed out behind me. Weird, huh?

A little.

Not long after this, I dream of Adrien. He's riding a black horse, powerful, like a steam engine: all nostril and hoof and tail. Adrien's wedding dress is long, flowing, beaded, many-layered. It billows behind and around him as he rides, and as the tempo of the hoofbeats quickens, the dress lengthens and widens until it covers first the horse, then Adrien himself, and finally, there is nothing but the bridal gown, huge and hurtling, ghosting across the fields, galloping on its own to a wedding it will know when it gets there.

*Lots of fags look down
on drag queens. They should
remember that it was mostly
drag queens who fought back
at Stonewall. If it wasn't
for them, where would
any of us be?*

HUNGER

On Sundays, before the show, the drag queens get together for a potluck dinner. Adrien cooks up a big pot of chili, and someone brings bread, and someone brings salad, and they all sit around and gossip and dish until it's time to put on the paint and roll on out to the hotel. Sometimes four people come; sometimes fifteen. It doesn't really matter. It feels like family.

The first time I go, I stop at the bakery and buy a chocolate mousse cake, frosted with pink goo and decorated with a sticky heart. It's just gone Valentine's Day, and if this confection doesn't find a home soon, it will meet a sorry end. It's late when I arrive, and the party has gathered a certain momentum.

Adrien and Wanda sit facing each other across a table that's sown with Ardell Fashion Lashes, Wet 'n' Wild Nail Color, stick-on nails, brushes for the application of various powders, eyebrow pencils, Clear Perfection Corrective Cosmetics, any number of lipsticks in any number of shades. The table is hardly wide enough to accommodate all these accoutrements, and their two lighted makeup mirrors. Their talk is animated and good natured at the beginning, when the roughing in is underway, when the beard lines are being masked. They've done all this a thousand times before. They could do it with their eyes closed. As the work progresses, and the fine detailing starts, they look at each other less and less. Their concentration and focus shift to the mirror: to the creation of the fairest of them all.

I ask the question I have to ask, even though I suspect there won't be a real answer, "Why?"

"This is not something I can choose not to do. This is something I have to do. This is something I have to do because this is who I am. Or who I want to be. Someone glamorous. Someone gorgeous."

"Ah."

I taught myself to sew when I was about eight. We had a mending pile that my mom never got around to. It got bigger and bigger. We were actually outgrowing the clothes before they got fixed, so I took over and started sewing on buttons.

Drag Tip 4

If your chest or legs start to
itch when the hair grows back
after shaving, swab the
affected area with baby oil.

Analytical, no. But show me the singer who can really
explain the impulse to release the thing that inhabits his
throat. The gift is to recognize the talent, and to have
the courage to set it free.

Adrien and Wanda make free with each other's stuff.

"Can I wear that brooch?"

"Have you still got that red wig, the one you bought
in Seattle?"

"Did you remember to bring that stole? The fox, I
mean."

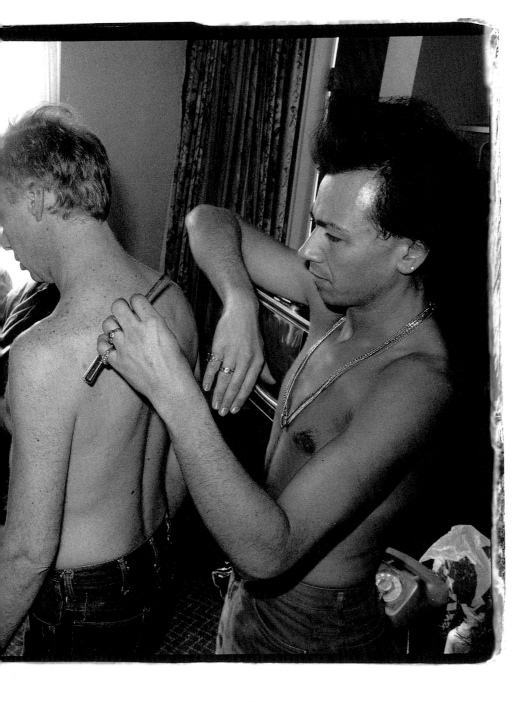

Adrien has designed a corset, which everyone in the room has examined and exclaimed over. It will sculpt his gut, and emphasize his chest. Squeezing into it proves a considerable challenge. We're all enlisted to help: pulling, lacing, tugging, encouraging. He puts on a little cocktail number he whipped up that afternoon. He is blonde tonight. Wanda is in a long black gown, tight, and slit to the thigh. Raven haired. Cabs are hailed. The party is over. They are off to become themselves.

I am left on the sidewalk with a thin young man who

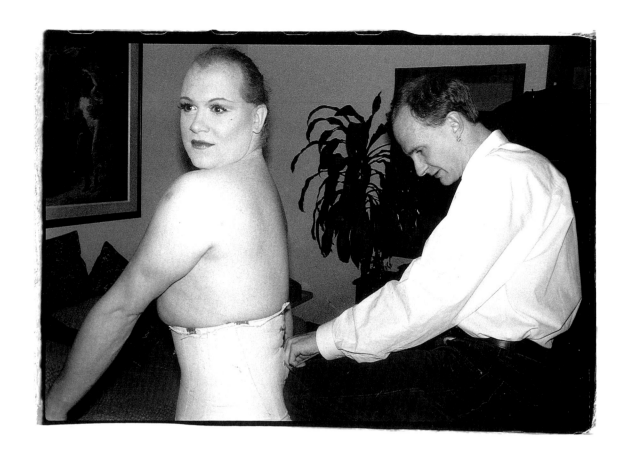

I can't even count the number of benefits I've
performed in over the last year. We've raised
money for AIDS, for sick kids, for the food bank.
There was a dying drag queen who wanted to go
back home to the east coast. It was the middle
of winter. She was broke: no coat, no long johns,
nothing. We put a show together and in just
under an hour we raised $700.03.

spent this potluck evening at the beck and call of the dressing queens, looking for lashes, helping with wigs, lacing the corset. He is quiet, and very sweet natured. I ask: "Do you do drag, too?"

"Sometimes. Not too often. My lover doesn't like me to. He can't understand why I'd want to dress as a girl."

"Ah."

"He's a realtor."

As if that explained everything.

A few weeks later, I see him at a club. He's in drag, and he's very beautiful. Very beautiful. And beaming. It takes me a few minutes to recognize him. Even before I do, I know I am looking at someone who, at that time and in that place, is not hungry.

*When the music comes on,
and the lights hit you—that's
a moment of glory. That's a
moment of suspension. That's
when it becomes spiritual.*

GLASS

One day, I learn the word "titivate": to make to look smart, to spruce, to adorn, to dress up. Colloquial, also spelled "tittivate." That same night, I say it out loud while watching Adrien at his makeup mirror.

"Titivate," I say to no one in particular. To the air.

He looks at me, arches a carefully pencilled brow, but says nothing. Tonight he has the look of one who is native to some exotic locale, and who barely tolerates tourists.

In my battered dictionary, titivate follows on the heels of titillate. It seems an apt pairing, especially in this instance. Adrien's makeup table is in the window of his ground-floor apartment, and the building is located just a few steps off one of the busiest corners in the city. He

I got an allowance like most other kids, but I used it to buy lipstick instead of candy. Now, my mom borrows my makeup.

rarely closes the Venetian blinds, and the ill-trimmed hedge affords no shelter from prying eyes. Anyone who cares to detach himself from the passing parade can watch the transformation. Some are amused, some are puzzled, some, no doubt, are put off. Most, for better or for worse, are titillated.

"Why don't you bother with the blinds?" I ask. This is the question of someone who closes the door to the bathroom when he's alone in the house.

"Mostly because I'm claustrophobic."

Drag Tip 5

Never drop your tips. But if you must for whatever reason, always have someone else pick them up for you.

This, frankly, I find hard to believe. But this doesn't seem like the night to be in any way confrontative.

"Do you always attract a crowd?"

"Always."

"Does anyone ever talk to you?"

"Oh, sure. I get women who want makeup tips. I get guys who want me to paint them so they can surprise their girlfriends. I get people who want to come into the apartment to watch. I get gay guys who've always wanted to try drag once and want me to make them up."

"How do you answer them?"

"Mostly, I ignore them. Why should I pay any attention? This is my home."

"But you also transform this window into a kind of theater."

"And this little mirror is part of my stage," he says. "But no one comes in here unless I ask them."

This sounds enough like a warning that I just sit back and watch quietly. This is a Dolly Parton kind of evening. Blonde wig piled high, a fluffy blouse, a black belt, and a checked farm-girl dress that started out as a tablecloth. Adrien puts on his lipstick, the proverbial crimson gash. He caps the tube, tosses it into his makeup box, and slams it shut. He looks at himself in the lighted mirror and makes a little face. It's been a bad day, I guess. And now, there's the night to contend with. He looks out the window, looks past his own pale reflection, out into the congregating dark, out past the one or two curious on-lookers who look back at him, through a glass, darkly.

When I started out, I had trouble with my tits slipping, with tuck coming loose. So I got advice from everyone. The other queens were always helpful. I think they were flattered to be asked. Flattery is one of the best ways to get on the good side of a drag queen.

ATTENTION

Andrew takes a break. He's sewing a beautiful gown: heavy black lace, jet beads, rhinestones, bugle beads. He's not making this elaborate confection for himself. It's for another queen to wear at an upcoming ball. Andrew makes most of his living by designing and sewing gowns. He's very fast, and very talented. About fifty percent of his output goes to drag queens. The rest of his clients are women. He gets a lot of referrals from his mother, a florist. She always asks a bride to be, when she comes in to order her flowers, if the dress is taken care of. If not, she gives her Andrew's number. I have seen Andrew's closet. I say, lucky the bride who finds him.

Andrew says, "For attention. I do it for attention. It took me a long time to figure that out. I'm the middle child of three. I was reading a book about the psychology of birth order, and it said that second children are often the attention seekers. That was me. That was me from the very beginning. I used some pretty extreme measures to try to get my parents to notice me. Like leaving the house in full drag when I was seventeen. I didn't even try to explain. Just headed out the door. They said, 'Where are you going?'"

What I like best, when I'm on stage, is spinning.
I can do toe spins, four in a row, without
stopping. That's why I wear three-inch heels.
They give me the freedom to move, they don't
hurt my feet. Then again, my feet really never
touch the ground.

I hate nails, and avoid them when I can. But they do finish the look. Stretch out your arm, extend your hand, and the nails make it look like your fingers go on forever.

" 'Out.'

" 'When will you be back?'

" 'Later.'

"Click click click went my heels down the street.

"It didn't do me a lot of good, as far as getting attention was concerned. After that, they stopped asking questions altogether. Anyway, ask a drag queen if she has any brothers or sisters, and five will get you ten you're talking to a second child."

Steven also says, "Attention. If you go to a club on a weekend, maybe six or seven hundred people will see you. At some point over an evening, every person in the place will focus on you. That feels good. It also feels good to know that you're giving them something, that you're making their night out a little less mundane than it would have been otherwise. I'm over six feet to begin with, and in seven-inch spikes, and with this huge hair, I add an extra foot to my height. No one can fail to notice."

I ask if he happens to be a second child.

When a tip comes from someone who you know for a fact doesn't have a lot of money, it's a real tribute. That's when you feel like you're doing a good job. And besides, it means you can buy a drink. We always remind the audience, "Remember! Tipping is not a city in China!"

"Yes. How did you know?"

I smile a sibylline smile, feeling a little like a circus carney who correctly guesses someone's weight.

Arin, a five-year veteran of the scene, and just turned twenty-one, says "Attention" without hesitation.

"Middle child?" I ask, smugly.

"First born," he says.

I should have known. Drag is nothing if not anti-formulaic.

"But what about the kind of attention you don't want? Do you get harassed in the street?"

"Never, knock on wood. Oh sure, there's an occasional catcall. But I've never been threatened. It's an in-

Drag Tip 6

Paint your nails before you apply them. You both color them and keep track of them easily by taping them to a piece of cardboard.

timidating sight, I think, a seven-foot queen in a leather jacket and thigh-high boots and not much else. I feel very safe."

Later that night, just after midnight, and I'm reading on the couch. I hear the telltale click click click of spike heels on pavement. I look from my window, three storeys up, and see the back of a queen I think might be Adrien, heading toward the clubs. All her sails are flying. Every head is turning. She's walking as if she doesn't have a care or fear in the world, as if she's man enough to handle anything and anyone she might meet along the way.

I used to have a terrible time
with shoes. They were expensive
and I could never get them in the
right size. Then I started shopping
at Frederick's of Hollywood.
Seven-inch heels and they
fit just fine.

CHANGELING

Carl is sitting opposite me in the coffee place, the day after his twenty-second birthday. I can't take my eyes off his eyes, one of which is blue. The other is brown. Is this so very unusual? Somehow, I think not. Still, I can't recall ever seeing it before, except in a wolflike dog who was once my neighbor.

Carl lives in a hotel downtown. Drag shows are popular there, and there have been times when the rooms above the bar have been occupied largely by queens who come to roost from one month to the next. Just at the moment, it's quiet. But Carl has seen whole hallways turned into dressing rooms, with much to-ing and fro-

After a while, you
learn there are
compromises you can
make and compromises
you have to avoid. I only
wear an outfit a couple
of times, so it doesn't
make sense to spend a
lot of money on it. But
it still has to look like
a million bucks.

ing, and banter and bitching and borrowing. He makes it sound like so much fun, so very festive, that I begin to imagine it as a sitcom.

Carl likes the hotel, although his room is very confining and there's a low-hanging light fixture with which he's forever colliding when working on a number. It's not that he's clumsy. Give Carl a stage, and it's a different story. He has that easy physicality that belongs to dancers and athletes. He has an agreement with gravity, and he can spin like nobody's business.

Carl comes from Newfoundland, and the lilting accent of that place sings through so clearly in his voice that it makes me sick with longing for everything I've had and known that's far away.

"Do I miss it? I don't miss the poverty. I don't miss the nosiness you find in villages like the one I grew up in. I miss the hospitality. And the spirituality. I think I'm a very spiritual person. But I just couldn't have stayed there. I couldn't stand the idea of how small my life would be. There was so much bottled up inside me, so much that needed to come out. That's why I love performing as much as I do. It's spiritual, too. There are times, during a show, when I feel like I'm not in control of my own body. I don't think I'm taken over or anything. But sometimes, when the lights hit you and the music comes up, it's so animating you could almost think you were channeling."

Carl grew up in the shadow of a hill that he says, only half-jokingly, was haunted. I think of his mother, wander-

ing around the rocks one day. She finds a sleeping baby
and brings him home. When he opens his eyes, she un-
derstands that he has been entrusted to her, and that
she has no way of anticipating his purpose here. All she
can do is raise him and let him go. She can set him loose
to dervish where and as he will, until he finds the people
who lost him. Until he comes home.

I have gay friends who are embarrassed to go with me if I'm shopping for women's shoes. I never have qualms. I go into mainstream stores to try on dresses. It's tempting to terrorize the sales clerks, and sometimes they get a little upset. But they get used to it. Mostly, they're very helpful.

Drag Tip 7

If perspiration is a problem under lights, finish off your face
by spraying it with hair spray. Close your eyes first.

ILLUSION

Andrew, who creates gowns for many of the city's queens, lives with a couple of roommates in an ordered and rather bland apartment in a run-of-the-mill highrise. Except for the gown he's beading when I arrive, there's nothing about the place that broadcasts drag queen. What did I expect? Wall-to-wall sequins? A "Cross-Dresser Crossing" sign on the street outside?

Andrew says, "I hate having heaps of drag around the place. I really try to keep my bedroom a drag-free zone, although I've got this huge Vegas showgirl headpiece in there now, sitting on my dresser. It's starting to ruin my sleep. I woke up tired this morning after I dreamed all

Drag Tip 8

If you're going to throw on a dress, don't be conventional. Be big. Never be run-of-the-mill.

night that I was working in some tacky lounge. The music was terrible."

Andrew shows me the headpiece, a towering and miraculous bird of paradise amalgam of feathers and beads and sequins. The remainder of the costume, he says, will only take a couple of hours to throw together.

"All I really need to finish it off is a dance belt, a bra, and some hot glue. I hate and despise hot glue. But sometimes it's useful."

Here's another reminder that I inhabit a very narrow world. It has never until this moment occurred to me that I might hold an opinion about hot glue, or that there are people whose minds are already made up on the subject and who will never be swayed.

I tell Andrew that I could never in a million years make something as elaborate as this headpiece, and he shrugs, shrinking a little, I think, from the praise. He looks at his work with the cool indifference a nanny might accord a homely baby.

I ask, "What do you love most about all this?"

"Seeing the work on stage. Looking around at an audience and knowing that they're stunned by something especially fabulous. Or that they've been fooled by an illusion. That's what this is about. Illusion. It's ninety-five percent illusion and five percent substance."

A few weeks later, I see Andrew at a big ball. He's wearing his headdress, and not much else. A wig. The bra. The decorated dance belt. The usual cosmetics, beautifully applied. He's a knockout, of course, and I feel very

Drag Tip 9

Tucking is the art of concealing the penis.
To tuck, pull the penis back, between your legs,
as far as it will go, parting the scrotum between
the testicles. Tuck your testicles up into their
cavities. Put on a dance belt. Then put on
your hose. Then apply another dance belt.
This way, the tuck will hold.
Tuck before you apply your nails.

shy of him. When I smile at him, he either doesn't recognize me, or doesn't see me, or chooses to keep on walking. He makes his way through a room of glittering queens, looking to see who's wearing his handiwork. He keeps on walking, certain that he's being watched, but more concerned with watching: watching to see who registers delight, fascination and outright awe when they come face to face with that which they know to be illusion, but which utterly takes them in.

What makes good drag? Great makeup
and a positive attitude. Being confident about
your outfit: no shoulder pads or tits spilling all
over. Good hair. By the time I'm ready to go out,
I've been over my makeup at least twice.
Everything has to be perfect. Otherwise, it's like
going to work and wondering all day if
you've left the oven on.

TAXI

How does it feel, the first time?

Arin says, "Painful. I knew nothing at all about sizing shoes. I wear a man's size nine. The first time I went out, I wore a woman's size nine that I'd tried to stretch for about two weeks."

Carl says, "Shocking. I was totally transformed. I never realized a dress and some paint could make such a difference."

Steven says, "Amazing. I didn't even like drag queens.

I thought they were horrible. I wasn't prepared at all for this veil of nelliness to settle over me. You really flounce. There seems to be a lot of hand action that comes into play, a lot of waving goes on. Amazing."

It seems that everyone who's meant to do drag knows instinctively how to act on a first foray, much as a whale born into the water knows just how to swim. I am astonished, time and again, to witness the shift that comes over these men when they slip into a frock and fix their eyes. They are so much changed that the only way they

Drag Tip 10

Drink beer through a straw.
It's easier on the lipstick.

can accommodate the difference is to grow and grow. Louder, smarter, funnier, ruder, bitchier. Of course. This is about broad strokes. This is about doing everything you can to make yourself seen. Why go to all this trouble if you're going to act as you would at home while watching videos?

Adrien and Wanda are walking down a busy street, with their attendants. I'm tagging along. The queens are both in very tight skirts, in very high heels, with very big hair, and very long lashes, and very impressive accessories. A bus passes, and every head turns on its stalk, like heliotropes rotating toward the sun. The queens wave and blow kisses. We walk past a crowded hotel restaurant, and every window-table conversation stops midstream. More kisses are blown. The queens are starting to crow.

"Hello! Hi! How are ya? Come down to the show! Oh my God in heaven, there's a man following us!"

And there is—a little drunk and weavy, it's true, but intent on his mission. There's a line of taxis outside the hotel. Adrien gives me a big kiss, and then the whole entourage jumps into one of the cabs. There's much clamoring, waving, and kiss blowing. They drive away, shouting something at their tipsy admirer, something I can't quite make out. Just as well.

I live only a few blocks away, but I'm sufficiently self-conscious about the huge lipstick stain on my chops that I don't want to walk there. So I get into the next cab.

The driver says, "Drag queens, eh?"

The question is rhetorical.

I ask if he often takes drag queens in his cab, and he pulls a little box from under the dash. It holds half a dozen sequins, some rhinestones, two lipsticks, an acrylic fingernail.

You don't dare to so much as think about doing Bette Midler in public until you've watched every movie, listened to every record, seen every concert clip you can. You study her gestures, her mouth, the arch of her eyebrow. You work and you work. You work for six months, maybe eight. Then, you might be ready.

"I found an evening glove, too."

I'm dabbing the lipstick from my mouth, and don't even think to ask just why he maintains this archive. Against what eventuality does he accumulate this evidence? Maybe for the same reason that I keep shiny stones and odd feathers I find on the beach: a tangible and pretty reminder of how the world's otherness, which we too often disregard, has passed our way and left its traces.

I've never been one for a routine lifestyle. I want the kind of life you can eat.

ASHES

Arin is sitting opposite me, facing the wall. It's mirrored, and he uses it to check things out. The comings and goings in the restaurant. His own face. He's articulate, young and worldly. He's twenty-one and has lived on his own for six years.

He says, "Here's my philosophy. Every fag can go to the bar. But it takes a fag with the nerve to turn up in a dress to really get the party going. It adds some excitement. And it's fun. Come in drag and you get a lot of attention, meet a lot of people. It's addictive. You can get lost in it. And that's how a lot of us start out: just showing up at clubs and parties, acting a little crazy, getting a reputation as a socialite. At the beginning, you

wear something you've borrowed, something ugly and very drag-queeny. On my first night I had on this frock with purple velvet sleeves, purple body, lots of beadwork and gold lamé ruffles. Definitely a starter gown, nothing I'd be seen in now. You can get along like that for a while. But eventually, if you're going to be serious about it, you have to do a show."

Arin quickly forsook the two-inch heels he wore on his maiden voyage for proper stilettos. And he threw himself into performing with uncommon gusto, sometimes mustering considerable forces to engineer baroque spectacles. One show featured a supporting cast of thirty-two leather men, thirty-two skinhead boys, and two dancing naked lesbians.

I held so much inside me for so long. It was all under pressure, waiting to come out. Now, it's being released, and I'm swimming in it!

How on earth would anyone find such a crew?

"Advertise," he says, with the shrugging nonchalance that belongs to those who see right through the impedimenta most of us spend our lives stumbling around or over.

Arin is a second-generation drag queen. One of his uncles, on his father's side, also had a distinguished career. This was not an oft-told family story. Arin's father approves neither of brother nor of son. But his mother is totally accepting, and often comes to see him perform. As does his brother.

I do it for fun. I do it for entertainment. I do it to get attention. Mostly, I do it because I'm really good at it.

Drag Tip 11

Remember that the
more you drink, the
more often you're
going to have to
untuck and tuck, while
wearing nails.

Drag Tip 12

To avoid losing a wig, "bobby pin it into next week." Also, a dab of nail glue on the temples will hold it in place.

"If I didn't have the support of my family, I don't know if I could do this. I'd have to hide so much. But my mom thinks it's great that I'll get out there and do the things I do. She's seen some pretty wild stuff. But she applauds like crazy and says to everyone around her, 'That's my boy!' She says that she's been blessed with a son and a daughter in a single package."

A couple of years ago, just after a particularly elaborate and trying show in which Arin performed a Madonna impersonation that garnered him considerable acclaim, he lost all his drag in a fire that started in the locker next to the one where he stowed his glamorous gear. Wigs. Gowns. Shoes. Bracelets. Beads. All gone.

"Thousands of dollars. Thousands. I could have sal-
vaged a few things. But looking at it there, soaked and
covered with soot . . . well, I just couldn't see the point.
So I started over. Started something new."

I want to ask: As easy as that? Just like any phoenix?
Instead, I watch his eyes drift to the reflecting wall, watch
him watch himself exhaling. He looks back at me, flicks
the ash off his cigarette, and smiles a smile that is more
inscrutable than anyone his age has a right to own. In it
I read: smoke and mirrors—that's all you need to know.

*We're cousins to clowns.
We shake things up. We hide
our surface selves with
makeup, and let what's
beneath come out. In drag,
I feel like I'm something more
than myself.*

MASQUE

Time goes by, and I start to see the bland quotidian in drag terms.

I look at women on the bus with unaccustomed interest, pay more attention to their nails, their hair, their makeup, their accessories. And sometimes i wonder: tucked? Why not? Several queens have told me about traveling to far-flung suburbs on public transportation, all decked out in full drag, very glam, and garnering appreciative stares from unsuspecting men. Nor are frumpish women, whose first allegiance is not to fashion, above suspicion. I think of Andrew's story.

"There was a big gay picnic in the park. It was after a pride parade. The police came along on their horses and

Mostly, I only know other queens by their drag names. When we see each other on the street, and we're dressed pretty straight, we stop and talk, but half the time I don't even know their boy names.

told us we'd have to move, that this picnic site had been reserved by the Miller family. Everyone argued back and forth for a while. There were several hundred gay people, and only half a dozen or so Millers. Finally, I marched up to this cop and his horse. I was wearing my overweight housewife drag. I put my hand on my hip and said, 'Okay.

Okay. I'm Mrs. Miller. And I say it's fine. Everyone can stay!'"

Which is not the kind of story you ruin by asking after the ending.

My relationship with language does a sideways shift. I begin to keep a list of everyday terms and phrases that

*I can never find the jewelry I like
in stores, so I've started making it
myself. A few pieces of filigree,
some beads, some rhinestones and
crystals and you have a gorgeous
pair of earrings for ten bucks.
I like it when the stuff looks
expensive but it's dirt-cheap.
Illusion. That's kind of the point.*

might make good drag names. April Showers. Lacy
Fringes. Elysia Fields. Virginia Creeper. Mable Syrup. Am-
ber Flashing. Rusty Bumper. Melba Toast. Crystal Gob-
lets. Candy Striper. Charlotte Russe. Probably, they've
all been used.

The day comes that I do a radio interview with Joan

Drag Tip 13

Breasts can be constructed in a number of ways.
Among the most popular: commercial breast
forms; bags filled with bird seed or rice;
balloons filled with a mixture of water and
gelatin; or any combination of these.

Collins. She's an actress whose on-screen bitchiness and exaggerated physicality have made her a staple in many a drag queen's repertoire. Joan is in town promoting a book called *My Secrets*. It features tips on health, comportment, and beauty maintenance. One of the moral mainstays of her mission is to point out that money is not a prerequisite for physical loveliness. For instance, you can have delicious skin well into your declining years if, instead of throwing away the peel of an avocado, you sim-

Drag Tip 14

Nail glue is also very useful for
holding big clip-on earrings in
place. Just use a drop, and
remove with a solvent.
Sometimes it makes your
lobes a little red.

ply take the thing and wipe it all over your body. One
may also maintain youthfulness by spending a couple of
hours a week reclining at home with one's face covered
in a mask of pulped bananas.

I find it hard to imagine Joan Collins lounging, poolside,
with her face thus adorned. Still, I read into this homely
advice the same ingenious rhinestones-into-diamonds
thinking that inspires so much dragcraft. And Joan her-
self, swathed in pelts, festooned with chains of gold, and
crowned with a very important wig, might just as well *be*
a drag queen. She has the same devotion to perfection,
the same superficial brassiness, the same evident vulner-

abilities, the same cagey intelligence. She is Joan Collins, The Product. Joan Collins, The Cartoon. She is Joan Collins, starring as Joan Collins. She is her own self twice removed, a masterpiece who begs imitation. No wonder her persona is so coveted.

A few weeks later, in another part of the country, I meet Mae Louise Campbell. She's an Ojibway woman, a maskmaker, who ran afoul of the local wildlife protection people because she used the feathers from a roadkill hawk in one of her creations. She shakes her head at the strangeness of it all. Now, to avoid ruffling anyone's plum-

age, she must make do with dyed goose quills. They work fine, too. Ersatz feathers, beads, bits of fur, odd and shiny scraps, paint. This is what she needs to make a mask: for ceremonies, for dancing, for erasure of the surface. As a poultice for what lingers not so very far beneath. She tells me this and I nod with recognition. This is what I've been hearing all along. Here is how the pieces fit. Now, everywhere I look, I see the possibility of transformation. Welcome to the world. Nothing here is sure except the erosion of certainties and, every so often, the sweet aching pang of surprise.

GODDESS

Adrien at his mirror, halfway to where he wants to be, hung eerily between guy and goddess, looks up and says, "Are you going to sleep with me?"

I can't tell, in that instant, if he's joking or making a serious proposition. How to parry? A curt no? Should I bat my eyes, and coyly lisp, "Why, we've only just met?" Instead, I let the question float for a few minutes, then ask if men ever fall in love with Miss Adrien.

"It happens. Sure, it happens. Men fall in love with Miss Adrien. She's everything boy Adrien wants to be: outgoing, outrageous, popular. Loved. But the thing is that Miss Adrien never appears in the bedroom. I'm proud

to say that I have never had makeup on my sheets. Miss Adrien gets left behind, she's washed down the drain at the end of the night. But she's who men fall in love with. She's who they want. So when she's gone, they usually walk out."

Adrien tells this story in a matter-of-fact way. It's straightforward, not at all melodramatic or self-pitying. Still, I find myself thinking, rather judgmentally, about how strange it must be to inhabit the same body as your arch-rival, to willfully create, night after night, the evil twin who always spoils the fun. What kind of pathology could this be? And furthermore, what planet do those men live on?

"So, are you going to sleep with me?"

"*No.*"

A chuckle.

That night at the club, Miss Adrien is emceeing the show. She starts out in a Reba McEntire getup, and will

---

My mom can't believe how careful I am with my makeup. She was over the other night and she asked why I was fussing with my eyelashes. I told her it's because the lashes really finish the look. They're wispy. They soften everything. Put on the lashes, and it all makes sense.

change at least twice over the course of the evening. There will be two sets, and six or seven drag queens will perform. The audience is small, but vocal. They hoot and holler when Miss Adrien says, "Here she is, a sweet little thing who's slept with everyone in the bar," or "Here she is, a real bitch, but we love her anyway." Standard patter. And when the queens perform their numbers, dancing and lip-synching to show tunes or current club favorites, their fans and followers and sometimes other drag queens come up from the audience and give them tips: a couple of dollars is the norm.

To avoid slipping on a
stage while wearing spikes,
make it tacky by spilling
some Coke on it.

Tipping is a weird and useful acknowledgment that fascinates me, largely because of the business attendant on it. Some of the queens reach out to take the bills without missing a beat, folding a graceful smile or nod into their number. Some break away from the song and have a small chat with the tipper. Others, swept away with artistry, refuse to acknowledge the fan, making him wait and wait until finally he just deposits his money on the stage, or pockets it and slinks off. Some queens take the money and let it fall with a pretence of heedless-ness, but look to some member of the entourage to re-

trieve it. Some insert it into their cleavage, some clutch it in their fists, others receive nothing at all.

Tipping a performer is not like sending a drink to a stranger, which is as anonymous an act as you care to make it. To tip a drag queen you walk to the stage. You stand in the lights. You become, for as long as it takes, a

Drag gives me an outlet to explore new looks, to always change, to be the way I'd like to be. I might not have a twenty-six-inch waist, but I can get one with a corset. I can have huge eyelashes and crazy hair. I can look retro or diva. I can be trashy or piss-elegant. I can vent all my crazy thoughts, and then go to work in the morning looking like me.

part of the performance, abandoning the safe faceless-ness that belongs to you as a member of the audience. For a shy person, it can be torture. I am very timid about this kind of thing, pathological even. I can't even bring myself to sing along at concerts. For that reason, rather than brute cheapness, I always hold back. This is a secret

shame: a small thing that has taken on disproportionate dimensions; an emblem of shabbiness or, worse, self-importance.

Miss Adrien leads off a set with the Gwen Verdon standard *All That Jazz*. She's hardly settled into the number before her fans and supporters are making their way to the stage with their folded bills. She smiles warmly at each one. The mood is so genial, the song so spritely, her bosom so ample, her mien so queenly, the room so warm, that I feel my reserve melt away. An altogether foreign current of courage courses through me. I walk

calmly, as though I have done this all my life, to the stage, and hand Miss Adrien the two dollars I have extracted from my wallet.

She spots the money first, squints through the lights to see who's offering it, smiles, reaches out for the tip, takes it, then leans down, sticks out her tongue, and licks me, sloppily, up the right side of my face. She winks broadly. Then she carries on, content with her offering. She's exactly where she wants to be and every inch a goddess.

What do drag queens want? To become legends.

ABOUT THE PHOTOGRAPHER

Born in the foothills of the Himalayas and schooled in Paris, France, longtime drag show fan Rosamond Norbury is an award-winning freelance photographer. Her acclaimed first book, *Behind the Chutes: The Mystique of the Rodeo Cowboy*, profiles the men who live up to the legends of the Wild West. It was nominated for the ALA/YALSA Best Books for Young Adults 1994 list. Her work has appeared in *Canadian Art* and *Saturday Night*, and has been shown in various galleries. When she isn't mountain climbing or touring Europe, she lives in Vancouver, British Columbia.

ABOUT THE AUTHOR

Distinguished writer and broadcaster Bill Richardson is the self-proclaimed Poet Laureate of Canada. His recent book, *The Bachelor Brothers' Bed & Breakfast*, won the prestigious Leacock Award for Humour. Previous books include *Come Into My Parlour, Queen of All the Dustballs*, and *Canada Customs*. Bill hosts CBC Radio's *Crossroads* and is a producer and frequent guest host for other CBC programs including *Gabereau*. He is also a regular columnist for *The Vancouver Sun* and *Western Living* magazine. Bill lives in Vancouver, British Columbia.

Photo credit: Ryan McNair